PROSPERO'S LIBRARY

The Book of
Love Symbols

PAVILION

The Book of Love Symbols
First published in Great Britain in 1994 by

PAVILION BOOKS LIMITED
26 Upper Ground, London SE1 9PD

A DBP Book, conceived, edited and designed by Duncan Baird Publishers
Highlight House, 57 Margaret Street, London W1N 7FG

Text: *Peter Bently*
Design: *Paul Reid*
Commissioned artwork: *Hannah Firmin*
Commissioned photography: *David Murray*
Picture research: *Julia Brown*

A CIP catalogue record for this book is available from
The British Library.

ISBN 1 85793 1432

2 4 6 8 10 9 7 5 3 1

This book may be ordered by post from the publisher.
Please contact the Marketing Department.
But try your local bookshop first.

Contents

Agents of love

Many divinities have been said to
preside over affairs of the heart. In ancient
Greece, the most famous was Aphrodite
(Venus to the Romans). Eros (Cupid), her
son, has much in common with Kama,
the Hindu love god: in both West
and East, love is an archer
whose arrows will reach even the
most resolute of hearts.

Aphrodite (Venus)
Aphrodite embodied all aspects of
sexuality. Her father, Uranos, was
castrated in a fight for supremacy
in heaven; she was born from
the sea at the place where his
genitals fell. The Romans
fused the goddess with
their own Venus, a
minor fertility deity.

Love's archers

Eros (left) is the winged messenger of love, whom the Romans called Amor or Cupid. Armed with a bow, he may be blindfolded, to show that love is blind. Kama (right) is a vigorous youth. He, too, is an archer, and flies on a parrot or sparrow, accompanied by honeybees, which symbolize the sweetness of love – and its sting.

Flaming heart

The burning heart, an attribute of Venus since the Renaissance, represents sexual passion and love's benign radiance. From China to ancient Mexico the heart has been revered as the seat of the emotions. However, as a love symbol it may be a stylized representation of the female genitalia.

Fortunes of love

Divination

Folklore is full of divination techniques for hopeful lovers. Catching the bouquet at weddings is familiar in the West, but there are more exotic ways to cast a romantic horoscope – from tracing the scurryings of spiders to rituals with handkerchieves.

Shooting star
In Italy, anyone who sees a shooting star on St. Lawrence's Night (August 10) will dream of the future beloved.

Nuts in May
A lover who throws hazelnuts on a log fire in May should watch closely: if the nuts crackle and fly apart, the romance will be passionate but short-lived.

Mistletoe
An old Welsh tradition claims that if an unmarried woman sleeps with a sprig of mistletoe under her pillow, she will dream of the man she will marry.

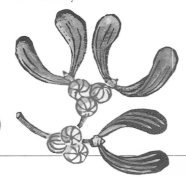

Garters

A woman who is abroad and knits a garter about her right stocking will, it is said, see her future husband in a mirror if she recites these words: "Far from home where I stay, may my destiny be told by my garter."

Myrtle

Myrtle, an evergreen shrub bearing white flowers, was sacred to the love goddess Aphrodite. In the Near East it was believed that if its leaves crackled when held in the hand, the one you loved would be yours forever.

Fortunes of love

Heavenly bodies

The heavens have held great significance for lovers since antiquity. The planet Venus was identified with the love goddess of the same name; its colour is green, the symbol of new life and young love. The stars were believed to determine the course of love: Romeo and Juliet, Shakespeare's "star-crossed lovers", are the most famous of all ill-fated couples.

Sun and moon

Just as the moon in most cultures stands for female sexuality, the sun is seen as male, the source of potency and growth. In astrology, the sun represents the desires of the heart. Its influence is greatest in the signs of Leo and Aries.

Ariadne's crown

The Greek hero Theseus, slayer of the
Minotaur, abandoned his lover
Ariadne on the isle of Naxos. She
was found by the god Dionysos,
who married her and gave her a
beautiful crown of red gemstones
and gold. It became the
constellation Corona Borealis
(Northern Crown; left), a symbol
of despair confounded.

Yin and Yang

In Chinese thought, the Yin
and Yang are the opposing
but interdependent forces
that govern the universe:
Yin is passive and feminine,
while Yang is active and
masculine. The illustration
shows the Yin-Yang symbol
and the symbolic animals
important in Chinese astrology.

Spells and potions

Belief in aphrodisiacs – foods, spells or potions taken to encourage amorous desires – is very ancient. In medieval legend, Lady Isolt and the knight Tristram unwittingly partake of a potion intended for Isolt and her betrothed, King Mark of Cornwall – with tragic consequences. Supposed aphrodisiacs have included even the tomato: 17th-century English Puritans condemned it for encouraging "immorality".

A witch's potion
Traditional witchcraft says that love potions should be made from plants associated with the planet Venus and the full moon. These plants should be picked at dawn and include elder flowers, violets, fennel and mint.

Honey
As well as being an aphrodisiac, honey was once said to impart fertility. The Mother Bee was another name for Demeter, the ancient Greek fertility goddess.

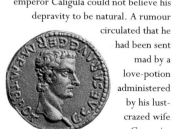

Mandrake

A narcotic root that often resembles the human body, the mandrake was once held to have magical and aphrodisiac properties. When it was uprooted, the plant was believed to let out a scream that brought death to the person holding it: for this reason it was customary to employ a dog to pull the root out.

Mad Caligula

Contemporaries of the Roman emperor Caligula could not believe his depravity to be natural. A rumour circulated that he had been sent mad by a love-potion administered by his lust-crazed wife Caesonia.

Seafood

The supposed aphrodisiac properties of seafood relate to its association with the sea-born Aphrodite. Oysters (above) symbolize the female genitalia, while shrimps and the like stand for the male sexual organs.

Strange loves

Mythology and folklore abound with mismatched lovers, such as the prince and the poor girl, as in the story of Cinderella, or the maiden and the monster, as in Beauty and the Beast. Often, these tales symbolize the triumph of love over social or physical differences. Sometimes, however, the stories can warn of the dangers of straying from conventional paths.

Mermaid
It was once said that sailors fell in love with mermaids, beautiful women with fishes' tails. Stories of mermaids may have arisen through misidentification of animals like the sea lion.

Beauty and the Beast
Tales of a maiden who falls in love with a monster show the value of true love: the maiden overcomes her repulsion and grows to love the beast for himself.

Achilles and Penthesilea

At the siege of Troy, the Greek hero
Achilles slew Penthesilea, queen of the
Amazons, a fierce race of women
warriors. At the precise moment of
her death, he fell in love with her.

Echo and Narcissus

As the nymph Echo pined away in unrequited love for the
beautiful Narcissus, she cursed him to fall in love with his
own reflection. He, too, pined away and was transformed
at his death into the flower that bears his name.

Flowers

The ancient Greeks and the Ottoman Turks each developed their own flower symbolism, a process continued by the 19th-century flower glossaries of Europe and America: some of the meanings given were new, but others harked back to ancient beliefs in the fruitfulness of nature.

Rose

In the West, the rose represents both the sweetness and, because of its thorns, the pangs of love. A red rose stands for passionate, carnal attachments. A white rose symbolizes pure, spiritual love: it is the emblem of the Virgin Mary.

Lotus

Associated in the East with the sun and moon, the lotus is a powerful symbol of love, light and life. In the West, where its nearest symbolic equivalent is the rose, it was once revered as the flower of Aphrodite.

Snapdragon

For most insects, it
is folly to approach the
snapdragon, because its
closed mouth yields to none
but the strongest of six-legged
suitors. The flower denotes vain
pursuit: a woman who gives it
to an admirer is telling him to
come no further.

Clover

The four-leaf clover (three
leaves are usual) is a lucky find: it is
a sign of love returned. In some country areas
its discovery was once taken as a sure sign that one
would soon meet one's future beloved.

Honeysuckle

This flower
entwines itself
around other plants
and represents the bonds
of love. It is associated —
wrongly, as bees do not visit it —
with honey, traditionally an
aphrodisiac.

Gifts of love

Love tokens

Jewels

Love jewelry has a language of its own. These garnets (left), like the anchor they accompany, signify devotion and loyalty.

Gifts between lovers were once governed by an elaborate code of etiquette. Traditionally, a gift of jewelry was respectable only if a couple was engaged: a young woman might give an admirer a lock of hair, but not if it were set in a jewel. In the 16th and 17th centuries, decorated scissors were popular: they symbolized two people joined as one and were also an exhortation to enjoy youth's pleasures before Fate cut the thread of life.

Lockets

Lockets, decorated with amorous emblems and inscriptions, have been popular since the Renaissance. They might contain a lover's portrait or a lock of hair. A locket symbolizes love firmly shut in the heart, especially if the locket itself is heart-shaped.

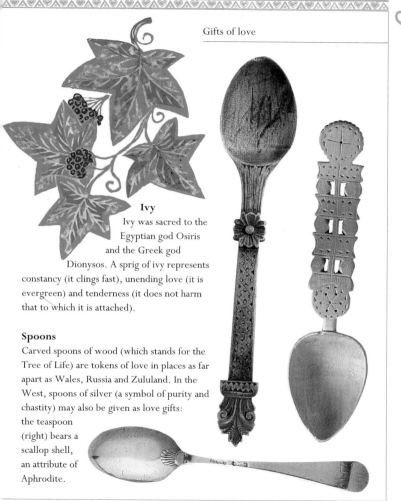

Ivy

Ivy was sacred to the Egyptian god Osiris and the Greek god Dionysos. A sprig of ivy represents constancy (it clings fast), unending love (it is evergreen) and tenderness (it does not harm that to which it is attached).

Spoons

Carved spoons of wood (which stands for the Tree of Life) are tokens of love in places as far apart as Wales, Russia and Zululand. In the West, spoons of silver (a symbol of purity and chastity) may also be given as love gifts: the teaspoon (right) bears a scallop shell, an attribute of Aphrodite.

Dress

From the blatant sexuality of the medieval codpiece to the coy invitation of the dropped handkerchief, the wide-ranging symbolism of clothes and other accoutrements has been exploited by lovers since ancient times.

Shoes

Shoes stand for both liberty and submission: in antiquity, only the master decided when the barefoot slave could wear shoes and go free. In parts of Europe a bride would throw a shoe to the groom to symbolize the transfer of male authority from father to husband.

Veils

The veil can be the seducer's mask, behind which lurk temptation, carnality and danger. The lifting of the veil at a wedding symbolizes the end of innocence and chastity.

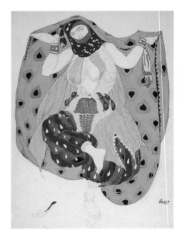

Sleeves

Detachable sleeves, adorned with ribbons or true-love knots, were commonly worn by lovers in the Middle Ages, perhaps because of their tubular shape (resembling both the male and female organs). Green, associated with spring and youth, was a popular hue, celebrated in the 16th-century English song "Greensleeves".

Fans

In China the fan symbolized the breath of life; when imported to Europe in the 16th century it kindled the flames of love. If a chaperoned young Spanish woman held a shut fan to her breast, she was telling her suitor: "My heart is yours!"

Gifts of love

Valentines

As a day for lovers, St. Valentine's Day has little to do with the two obscure 3rd-century Christian martyrs of that name who are commemorated in the church calendar on February 14. The occasion derives in fact from pagan fertility festivals of the early spring, such as the Roman Lupercalia, which took place on February 15.

Crocus
Traditionally held to bloom on Valentine's Day, the crocus heralds the arrival of spring. It also symbolizes the carefree happiness of young love.

Gloves and gauntlets
The most common Valentine's Day gift from the 17th to the 19th centuries, gloves or gauntlets stood for honesty (clean hands) and friendly intentions (offering a gauntlet meant the hand bore no weapon).

Birds

Valentine's Day was once called the Birds' Wedding Day, from an old belief that this was when birds chose their mates. Hence the custom of inviting someone to be your "mate" or Valentine, originally just for the day.

Cards

Possibly the first ever greeting cards, Valentine cards originated in the 16th century and reached the height of exuberance and sentimentality in the Victorian age. They are adorned with love symbols, especially hearts and Cupids.

Shells

Seashells are attributes of the love goddess Aphrodite (Venus), who rose from the sea. Traditionally, they often decorated the gifts exchanged by Valentines.

Love knots and rings

A love knot, like a ring, is a symbol of eternal union – the voluntary entangling of lifelines. What is implied is not servitude, but a wholehearted welcome to the ties of mutual destiny. One form of this emblem is the bow, which represents the love knot as a luxury proudly worn. In Japan, love letters (left) were traditionally sent on pieces of paper folded and tied in a knot.

Garlands
A love token symbolizing the lightest and most carefree of entanglements – and an honest recognition that the flowers of love may quickly fade. The message is simple: seize the day!

Blue ribbon
A blue knotted ribbon is traditionally worn by lovers. Blue, the colour of the Virgin Mary, represents a love that goes beyond sexual attraction.

Eternal knot
The endless knot signifies both eternal love and longevity – implying that a happy union may bring long life.

Rings

Rings are a symbol of the love that, like a ring, has no end. However, the Puritans who ruled England in the 1640s tried – in vain – to ban the wedding ring as "a diabolical circle for the Devil to dance in".

Yellow ribbon

Yellow symbolizes the sun, light and goodness, and is a colour of fidelity and constancy. In the United States, to hasten the return of an absent loved one, yellow ribbons are traditionally worn or fastened to part of the home or to a tree (such as an oak, which stands for strength in adversity).

Chivalry

The knightly ideal of chivalry placed honour, courtesy, sacrifice and chastity above physical love. A classic exemplar of these values was Sir Thomas Gresham, an Elizabethan courtier, who once powdered down a priceless gem, mixed it with wine — and drank the health of his beloved queen.

Forget-me-not
German legend tells of a knight who drowned while picking a flower for his lady. His spirit lives on in the flower, which is called after the knight's dying words: "Forget me not!"

Maiden in the tower
A common subject of folk tales is the maiden shut in a tower (to protect her virginity) and rescued by a hero. The tower stands for purity and femininity; it is also a phallic symbol, denoting male control.

Unicorn
This fabulous beast was an emblem of the chivalric ideals of spiritual love and feminine chastity. Only a virgin, it was said, could capture and tame the creature.

The lady's colours
In battle or at a tournament, a medieval knight would sport his beloved's colours for good luck
– in the conquest both
of his adversary
and of his
lady's heart.

Temptation

A seduction may be slow and insidious, like the approach of a snake, or sudden and overwhelming, like a pirate assault. Round, succulent fruit may also symbolize sexual temptation: they have ancient associations with female sexual organs and fertility.

Serpent

The serpent is associated with the phallus and with hidden and possibly sinister lusts: this is the beast that tempted Eve with the fruit of the tree of knowledge. But as a denizen of the earth the serpent can also symbolize fertility.

Torch

The flaming torch is an attribute of Aphrodite and Eros, who were said to use it to kindle the fires of passion. In Western art, an extinguished torch often stands for a failed seduction.

Ship of love

The Greeks sometimes compared the heart struggling with the temptations of love to a ship wracked by storms or assailed by pirates. A magic ship was an attribute of Freyja, Norse goddess of love and marriage.

Apple

The Bible does not name the fruit with which Eve tempted Adam: its identification with the apple may derive from ancient mythology. Paris of Troy, asked to give a golden apple to the fairest goddess, chose the seductive Aphrodite, whose attribute the apple became.

Swan

The swan is a symbol of seduction on account of its shape (it resembles the ancient image of the winged phallus). In Greek myth, Zeus took the form of a swan to seduce Leda, Queen of Sparta. Two swans drew the chariot of Aphrodite.

Passion and arousal

The symbolism of sexual passion often draws upon the animal kingdom for images of potency with the added suggestion of lower instincts. The goat is one such symbol: it is linked with dark forces (the Devil, it was believed, often took a goat's form) and sexuality (goats drew the chariot of Eros). Pan (left), the Greek god of carnality and chaos, is usually depicted as part goat.

Lingam* and *yoni
These ancient Hindu totems represent sexual love and passion. The phallic *lingam* represents arousal, creation and renewal. The *yoni*, its female counterpart, is passively receptive.

Swallows
The swallow can symbolize sexual arousal, perhaps because of the vaginal associations of its V-shape. The bird was sacred to Aphrodite.

Ball in cage
A symbol of the soul imprisoned by love and of passion restrained, the caged ball is a common decorative motif: it occurs on love spoons.

Wild horse
The untamed or winged horse is an appropriate emblem of unbridled passion. For the ancient Celts the horse was the companion of Epona, the goddess of fertility. In the art of the Renaissance the animal became a symbol of lust.

Moods of love

Love in jeopardy

The many pitfalls of love have produced a wide range of symbols, from the yellow carnation (expressing unreciprocated love) to the fox (a creature associated with deception and betrayal). In some rural areas, it was once considered an omen of quarrels ahead for a couple if they both looked into a mirror at the same time.

Green knot, yellow rose
Being given a yellow rose or a green knotted ribbon means that your love is rejected. Both pale green (decay) and dark yellow (the setting sun) imply the death of love.

Cuckoo

The cuckoo is a common symbol of the husband rejected for another. It usurps the nests of other birds, and in France and England the "cuckoo" ("cuckold" is derived from the same word) was originally the adulterous interloper. Later the word was applied to the hapless husband, perhaps because a cuckoo's odd nesting habits have also made it a byword for foolishness. In Japan, the bird stands for unrequited love.

Green-eyed jealousy

In Shakespeare's *Othello*, the villain Iago calls jealousy "the green-eyed monster, which doth mock the meat it feeds on." This may refer to the disdainful cat, whose loyalty is not bought by food. Jealousy is said to turn its victims green.

Reconciliation

Among the most ancient symbols of reconciliation and harmony restored is the dove bearing an olive branch in its beak. A gift of nemophila may speed the process of making up: this plant expresses forgiveness. Another flower, the golden tuft alyssum, which was once believed to cure disease, represents the healing of a rift between lovers.

Clock

Time heals all ills: no matter how far apart they are, a clock's hands always come back together. The 19th-century German clock (above) is adorned with love emblems such as Venus and roses.

Hazel

Hazel blossom denotes love reconciled. The symbolism is ancient: the Celts revered the hazel as a tree of wisdom and peace, and Hermes, the Greek god of reconciliation, carried a hazel wand.

Broken sword
As the sheathed sword is traditionally an emblem of
peace, the broken blade stands for forgiveness and
making up: it represents the destruction of whatever
has wounded the heart.

Phoenix
The phoenix, a fabulous bird
once said to inhabit Egypt
or Asia, is a symbol of
life and love renewed.
According to myth,
the creature lived
for centuries.
At the end of
its life it
settled on a
pyre, which it
set ablaze by
beating its
wings: it was
reborn at the
very moment it
perished in the
flames.

Love fulfilled

Constant affection

he many emblems of everlasting love range from
evergreen plants, such as the ivy and laurel, to creatures
such as the dove (a pair of doves denotes conjugal
harmony and devotion). A sapphire (left) was
once believed to ensure fidelity because it
would turn from dark to pale blue if a lover
was unfaithful.

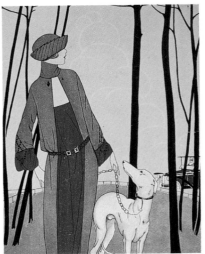

Faithful dog
In Europe and China the dog
has long been a symbol of
unconditional love and trust.
In Western portraits, a dog at
the sitter's feet traditionally
represents marital fidelity.

Bluebell
Blue flowers, such as the bluebell (below) and violet, symbolize the depths of true love. Blue was associated in ancient Greece with the goddess Hera, protector of marriage and fidelity.

Laurel
In parts of Europe the laurel was once believed to deter lightning, which splits things in two. A couple would each pin half of a laurel sprig to their clothes to show their constancy.

Chain and anchor
Many symbols are inspired by the idea of the soul as a ship on the sea of life. The chain and anchor signify constant love, steadying the heart against life's tempests.

Love fulfilled

Weddings

Awedding marks the beginning of a new life: Russian brides-to-be once wore mourning to mark the passing of maidenhood. Many Western wedding customs derive from ancient practices designed to ensure the fertility of the couple.

Bells

In Europe, the bride and groom were once believed to undergo a literal rebirth during their wedding. Bells were rung to ward off evil at the vulnerable moment of transformation.

Cakes and confetti

Wedding cakes have their origins in the small cakes once baked as fertility offerings to the bridal pair. The first confetti were grains thrown to ensure the bride's fruitfulness.

Dress

In the Christian tradition, red (denoting both loose morals and martyrdom) and green (envy) are avoided for a wedding outfit. However, in China, these colours are auspicious: the groom's jacket (left) bears lucky motifs such as the butterfly.

Flowers

Boutonnieres (buttonholes) originated in the gifts or "favours" given to wedding guests for good luck. In Normandy, red rosettes were attached to bridal carts to ward off witches.

Horseshoe

A horseshoe, it is said, has been given to newlyweds ever since Satan went to have his hooves reshod. The smith turned out to be St. Dunstan, who tortured Satan until he promised to enter no house displaying a horseshoe.

Fertility

Most ancient civilizations sought ways to ensure a couple's fruitfulness. In particular, many plants (such as the mandrake) were said to enhance fertility; others, such as lettuce or parsley, were thought to render a wife infertile if she grew too many of them.

Egg

The egg is an ancient fertility symbol. Its association with Eastertide derives from the pagan Germanic belief that birds laid their eggs around the time of the spring equinox.

Cornucopia

The mythical Cornucopia, or Horn of Plenty, is said to dispense unending bounty to its possessor. It was said to come from Amalthea, the goat that suckled the god Zeus: in antiquity a goat's horn was said to bestow fertility.

Moon

The menstrual cycle gives the moon great significance as a symbol of female fertility. To most peoples the moon itself is seen as female, though in some areas it is associated with male potency – for the Maori, the moon is "every woman's husband".

Corn dollies

In parts of Europe it was traditional to make a female doll from the last sheaf of wheat harvested. It hung in the kitchen until the following year to bring fruitfulness and prosperity upon the farmer and his household.

Rabbits and hares

These most productive of mammals are linked with the moon as symbols of female fecundity and are attributes of the goddess Aphrodite (Venus). They were associated with ancient spring fertility festivals.

Acknowledgments

The publishers are grateful to the following for permission to reproduce their objects and photographs:

Key: b: bottom c: centre l: left r: right t: top

Title page: And Seraphin, London; **Contents page**: Masada Antiques, London; **p.4-5**: Casa di Venere, Pompeii/Scala, Florence; **7**(br): A.P. Patterson/Ardea, London; **9**: Charles Walker Collection, London; **10**: private collection, London; **11**(tl): Charles Walker Collection, London; **11**(bl): private collection/The Bridgeman Art Library, London; **12**: (*Bottom Asleep* by G.F. Watts) The Fine Art Society, London/Bridgeman Art Library, London; **13**(l): The British Museum, London; **13**(r): (*Narcissus* by P.J. Redouté) Linnean Society, London/The Bridgeman Art Library, London; **14**: (*Lotus* by Yun Shou-P'ing) Osaka Museum of Fine Arts, Japan/The Bridgeman Art Library, London; **15**: (*Day Dream* [detail] by D.G. Rosetti) Victoria and Albert Museum, London/Bridgeman Art Library, London; **16**: (t,c,b) Masada Antiques, London; **17**: private collection, London; **18**(c): private collection, Oxford; **18**(b): (costume design for *Sheherazade* by L. Bakst) Fitzwilliam Museum, Cambridge/The Bridgeman Art Library, London; **19**(t) (*Portrait of a Lady* by F. Ubertini) private collection/The Bridgeman Art Library, London; **19**(b): private collection, Oxford; **20**: Cheltenham Art Gallery and Museum, Gloucestershire/The Bridgeman Art Library, London; **21**: private collection, London; **23**(c): private collection, London; **23**(cr): Masada Antiques, London; **23**(cb): private collection; **24**: (The City of the Soul, Ms.137/1687 f.182v) Musée Condé, Chantilly/The Bridgeman Art Library, London; **25**: (Luttrell Psalter, Add. 42130 f.202v) The British Museum Library, London/The Bridgeman Art Library, London; **29**: Stephen Dalton/N.H.P.A., Sussex; **32**: Bonhams, London/The Bridgeman Art Library, London; **34**(t): Bonhams, London/The Bridgeman Art Library, London; **34**(b): John Jesse, London/The Bridgeman Art Library; **37**: private collection, London; **38**: private collection, London.